Marketplace

MISSION
TRIP

A Six-Week Mission Trip to Your Workplace

"The Marketplace Mission Trip is an opportunity to be very intentional about every single step of your day, providing God's love on a personal level."

—**JANE TRAPMAN**, author, writer, and entrepreneur

"It's a great way to remind you to always be ready for Jesus to use you at any moment."

—**ZACH ROWELL**, director of customer relations

"I love the mission trips. They have opened my eyes to ways I can demonstrate my faith at my workplace, and my Follower of One friends supported me as I started a Bible Study at my school."

—**AMY WITHERS**, teacher

"Everywhere we go, God is calling us to be a missionary. I just love the fact that all types of people, no matter what industry they're in, are on a mission. You can share the gospel in so many different ways. I love it and support it!"

—**KEITH DAVIS**, missions pastor

"The simple curriculum of the *Marketplace Mission Trip* teaches that being a witness for Christ is as much or more about your actions and behavior as it is the words you say. I have become so much more confident and relaxed when it comes to sharing my faith because of the Marketplace Mission Trips."

—**BRIAN CYRIER**, company president

"I think this is a beautiful, important ministry pursuit. It helps believers understand that their walk with God is a daily process. [The mission trip] helps Christians recognize that their job has a divine purpose…"

—**CHRIS WALL**, senior pastor

"Love this idea!"

—**JESSICA FLETCHER**, supervisor for 911 dispatch

"Fulfilling our Lord's commission to go and make disciples doesn't take months of planning and travel to a foreign country. The *Marketplace Mission Trip* shows you how to get started bearing fruit where you work. You'll be amazed at how many opportunities you have to witness and help people in your space."

—**EMORY ROWLAND**, editor

"I've participated in the Marketplace Mission Trip a couple of times, and I'm convinced it has changed the way I lead my company, work with my staff and live my faith out in front of them."

—**PAGE COLE**, business owner

"We're big fans of Follower of One. They understand how difficult it is to share our faith in an increasingly secular world. The practical lessons, applications, and challenges give us a realistic understanding of how to share our faith at work (and honestly, anywhere)! There's no one else out there doing it quite like them!"

—**HUNTER WADLINGTON,** missions associate

"It pushes you to show up in a more conscious way during the workday with Jesus."

— **ED SAMUEL**, career coach

"This is a good reminder that we should take God with us to work every day. The five steps will help you put God into your everyday routine."

— **SCOTT GRAYBILL**, fire captain

"This Mission Trip made conversations easier to have. It also showed me that just praying for my co-workers and my students can go a long way to feeling Christ's presence in the school as a whole."

— **JOANN GARCIA**, teacher

"It helps me stay mindful of the fact that I can be the hands and feet of Jesus everywhere I go."

— **NICK NELSON**, CEO

"[This] was absolutely a wonderful daily reminder to be focused on Christ in those tasks rather than simply accomplishing the task."

— **TRISH BOONE**, vice president

"I haven't been able to stop talking about the Mission Trip. This will lift your spirit and give you a fresh sense on how God wants to use you."

— **BRENT VAWTER**, Oklahoma area director

"It helped me keep my focus on praying for my coworkers daily. And it helped me mentally prepare myself each morning."

—**NICK HAMILTON,** IT auditor

"The trip was a wonderful wake up call to bring my faith into my daily work life."

—**DOUG EDGAR,** entrepreneur

"I love the *Marketplace Mission Trip*! It helps me to remember that I can make a difference in the lives of the people I come in contact with every day, and that every interaction, big or small, is a part of my journey and an opportunity to grow myself and help others."

—**MARY DEAN,** project manager

Marketplace MISSION TRIP

A Six-Week Mission Trip to Your Workplace

MIKE HENRY SR.

HIGH BRIDGE BOOKS
HOUSTON

Marketplace Mission Trip
by Mike Henry Sr.

Printed in the United States of America
ISBN: 978-1-954943-51-3

High Bridge Books titles may be purchased in bulk for educational, business, fundraising, or sales promotional use. For information, please contact High Bridge Books via www.HighBridgeBooks.com/contact.

Published in Houston, Texas by High Bridge Books

Contents

Introduction

Congratulations! You've decided to embark on a six-
week exercise to answer the question, "How would a missionary do my job?"

On most mission trips, we go someplace, perform some service through which we visit with people and establish relationships to demonstrate our love of others and possibly share about Jesus. We pray for everyone we'll meet and the interactions we'll have. We genuinely want to make a difference both in their environment and in their eternal lives.

How This Guide Is Organized

For the next six weeks, you will take a mission trip to your regular job or your everyday activities. Each week, in group discussion, you'll cover a key idea or activity to do your job like a missionary.

After the session, there will be five daily verses with suggested activities, one for each day of the following work week. We encourage you to examine the passage and activity daily and make notes at the end of the day to discuss when your group gathers again. You may want to call a friend to discuss and pray for one another during this time.

These daily activities take place for six weeks. Over that time, you will lay the foundation for a habit to go into your daily mission field (workplace) with an action plan!

But remember, you're being paid to go on this mission trip. You don't have to burn any vacation or pay for any travel.

Initially, this may seem like a lot of work. It may be difficult for you to establish the daily habit of praying for people and looking for ways to serve them. We have years, maybe even decades, of habits already established.

But remember, you're being paid to go on this mission trip. You don't have to burn any vacation or pay for any travel. Simply spend a few minutes each morning in prayer. Ask Jesus to use you to bless the people you'll meet. Then, do what he says.

Similarities to Other Mission Trips

On this mission, we will go to our workplaces for the same purpose as an overseas mission trip: to establish relationships and help others move closer to Jesus. Maybe the people we work with already follow Jesus. Great! Let's help them move closer to him. Or maybe they don't follow Jesus at all. They may even harbor anger or other issues regarding our faith.

Without harming our working relationship, our goal is to help them move closer to Jesus, too. The person we're interacting with always has a choice. We want to make a difference that would cause them to question their own beliefs.

Differences from Other Mission Trips

The basic differences include your compensation, vacation, and travel. You will receive your normal compensation. You do not have to raise support, arrange travel, get shots, or use vacation days to take part in this exercise. In addition, there are five key differences.

Difference #1: How You Do Your Job

You will be challenged to use your spare time, energy, and resources to go beyond what you normally do in your job. You can't deliver less work while you're on the mission trip. Your energy praying for and serving others needs to come out of your personal time. So, plan to come in a little early or work late. Your extra energy will be rewarded.

Difference #2: Long-Term Relationships

You won't be leaving when this trip is over. So, you must maintain your relationships. Resist the temptation to "force" a conversation or engineer circumstances to help Jesus out. He's in charge, and everything will happen in his time. Your work outcomes should improve because you're on a mission trip. Don't waste time, yours or anyone else's. Work to make others and your company successful. Making others ultimately, eternally successful is your earthly priority during this "trip."

Difference #3: Normal Routines May Become a Distraction

Even overseas mission trips have distractions. On this mission trip, your enemy will first distract you with your normal routines. You may find yourself busier than you expect or asked to do some work differently than normal. You will get interrupted. Even your interruptions will get interrupted. The world, our habits, and the devil all work to distract you and keep you from focusing on our relationship with Jesus.

Make sure you have a family member or friend praying for you and checking with you daily during this trip. Otherwise, one day you will realize several days have passed since you engaged with Jesus or the mission trip content.

Difference #4: More Spiritual Warfare Than Usual

Opposition from demonic forces happens on mission trips, too. But on a marketplace mission trip, it shows up in different ways. Trouble sleeping causes you to oversleep and arrive late for work. Or you experience depression, doubt, or frustration more than usual. Participants have experienced the death of a family member, or their company has been reorganized. You may have to stay home because of a sick child or another reason. In the years we've been running these trips, many extreme things have been reported. The enemy will try to knock you out of your routine.

Prayer is the best answer. Continue to pray that God will protect you and others on this trip. Ask family members and friends to pray for you, too.

Difference #5: More Discouragement Than Usual

Discouragement is no stranger to normal mission trips either. But now, you may face discouragement as part of your regular job. You may have a nagging sense of being unqualified. You might hear negative voices telling you this isn't working or your actions don't matter. You may wonder how you could be so foolish as to think something amazing would happen.

But stick with the daily activities and begin to build the habits. As you pray and interact with others on the "trip," these voices will quiet over time.

How This Works

Each week there is a brief video, a devotional, group discussion questions, and five action steps to be completed during the following week.

You agree to:

1. Read the devotionals and watch the videos.

2. Prayerfully consider each daily activity and make notes if desired.

3. Pray for the others in your group who take part in this activity.

As a group, decide if you will read the lesson and watch the video before or during your meeting. For weeks two through six, plan to review any notes, questions, or thoughts from the previous week before shifting the conversation to the current week.

Work through the discussion questions as a group. The five action steps are designed to be completed daily. Use the space for notes or a journal to record your thoughts, whether you want to share them with your group or keep them to yourself.

Leader's Notes

Throughout this guide, we'll insert notes for leaders to help you lead and encourage the group. Begin each day praying for every member of your "trip." Please be available for others, too. Share contact info and consider sending daily text messages or emails to encourage everyone to engage in the daily activities. We have an enemy who will work actively to resist our efforts.

Begin each week with your small group meeting. For meetings after the initial meeting, begin with prayer followed by a conversation about the previous week. What notes were made? What questions came up?

Then, move into the discussion for this week. Watch the video and go through the discussion questions with your group. Larger groups may want to break into smaller groups of three to five to give everyone a chance to talk. Leave time to discuss your answers. And close each session with a prayer. Ask each member to commit to the exercises again the following week.

Each day, pray for your group members. Ask God to help them read the verses, pray through the action item listed, and make notes.

Outcomes

One final note. Many end the trip and feel a little discouraged. They don't think much happened during their mission trip. This is especially true in the two-week version of the mission trip. After all, a workday is a workday. On ordinary workdays, little happens besides work.

Each day of your mission trip will be an ordinary day; you may see very little spiritual activity. But don't give up—look closer. Jesus and God, the Father, are working

(John 5:17), and the Holy Spirit is working too. When we get to work, they're already there, and they'll be there when we leave. God wants every person to know him better. We're simply upping our game!

Notes About This Book

Testimonies and stories in the book are used with permission, but the names of individuals, other than myself, have been changed.

Testimony From the Company Gym

Sue took the trip and recounted a meeting on Wednesday morning. Anne, a peer in the meeting, was particularly critical of a key project Sue was leading. But because Sue was on the mission trip, she decided not to fire back. She decided instead to listen to learn. She received the comments, suggestions, and ideas without any type of sharp response toward Anne. Later in the day, in the company gym, Sue was in the yoga class with only the instructor present. Anne walked in and joined the class. Because Sue listened and wasn't defensive, she and Anne had a much better conversation, and their relationship improved.

Expect God to Show Up!

You may not notice God working in your life. God seldom shows up out of nowhere. Often his work takes time. Your actions are like seeds. God will make them grow over time.

To deal with the discouragement, spiritual warfare, distraction, and relational challenges, plan to pray. Ask

God to watch over you, your family, and your coworkers, and expect this to be more difficult than usual. Ask him to keep your involvement in the mission trip front of mind. Do the daily work, and check in with the others in your group. Your investment will make this trip special. If you do not give up, you will see God work, and you will receive a reward (1 Cor. 3:14).

Daily Reminders

1. **Avoid sharing about this mission "trip" on social media or in your workplace.** You don't want your friends and coworkers to feel like an experiment. Limit your sharing to your group of close personal friends who will pray for you.

2. **Even when you ask a friend to pray, don't share others' names or circumstances.** Protect their privacy. If you ask someone in your small group to pray, ask them to pray for you. Then, you pray for your friends and coworkers. No one else needs the details. Keep all confidences.

3. **In everything, put others ahead of yourself. Give your life away** (Matt. 16:25).

Remember, this is between you and God. Guard others' privacy and be sensitive to their feelings. You work with these people. Trust God, and don't do anything to strain your work relationships.

Action Steps (Either Before or During the First Meeting)

1. Talk and pray with another person from your group during the week. You will be more engaged if you interact with others on this journey in between each meeting.

2. Ask God to bless, use, and protect each person in your group throughout the trip.

3. Begin praying for everyone you meet each day.

Notes and Prayer Requests

_____

_____

_____

_____

_____

_____

_____

_____

_____

_____

Marketplace **Mission Trip**

My Contacts

Name	Mobile Number or Email

Week One

Who Are We?

Leader's Notes

Introduction: Mike's Story

What does God expect from us at work? Does God expect less of us because we don't work for a church? When I first decided to follow Jesus, I struggled with this. I wanted a job following Jesus so I could be a full-time Christian. I didn't like my job. I wanted to work with the great Christian people I met. I wanted my faith to matter full-time.

Have you ever wondered if all you're supposed to do is stay out of trouble, donate money, and volunteer when you can?

Video

Begin the session by watching the video titled "Jesus's Job for Me." Then begin by asking members of your group to read the verses and discuss the questions below.

Matthew 5:16: Whose Light?

Early (and possibly often) in Jesus's ministry, Jesus calls "us" salt and light (Matt. 5:13–16). He ends by saying, "[L]et your light shine before others, so that they may see your good works and give glory to your Father in heaven" (Matt. 5:16 CSB).

Notice how the light, the good works, and the Father are all "ours." "Your light … your good works … your Father." It's our light because Jesus allows his light to be colored by each of us. They're our good works because we're the ones doing them. And God is our Father because we follow and obey Jesus.

Mark 10:42–45: Service or Ministry

Occasionally, Jesus's disciples got into arguments about which one would be the greatest. Once, Jesus corrected them with these words:

> And Jesus called them to him and said to them, "You know that those who are considered rulers of the Gentiles lord it over them, and their great ones exercise authority over them. But it shall not be so among you. But whoever would be great among you must be your *servant*, and whoever would be first among you must be slave of all. For even the Son of Man came not to be *served* but to *serve*, and to give his life as a ransom for many." (Mark 10:42–45, emphasis added)

What Is a Minister?

Three Greek words (*diakoneo, diakonia,* and *diakonos*) are used 100 times in 89 verses in the New Testament. Do those words sound familiar to you? They're the words translated as "servant," "served," and "serve" in the passage above. They're also translated as "deacon" or "deacons" six times (1 Tim. 3:8–12). They're translated as "servant" or "service" and "minister" or "ministry" most of the remaining 94 times.

A minister is a servant. Jesus came to minister, to serve, not to be served. We often call someone a "minister" because they teach about Jesus and they work for a church. But the word "ministry" simply means that we serve others so that Christ may be visible. Those who follow Jesus serve.

John 14:12

But did Jesus really say we would all "serve" or minister? He doesn't really say that here, after all. Right?

Well, after Jesus washed the disciples' feet at the Last Supper, he had a conversation with the 12 disciples to launch them into their ministries after he was gone. At one point, he said, "Truly, truly I say to you, whoever believes in me will also do the works that I do; and greater works than these he will do, because I am going to the Father" (John 14:12).

The work Jesus just completed was the most menial, low, servant work of that day. Then he went on to say that they would do "greater works." What do you think he meant by "greater works?"

I think the "greater works" means we will be able to be in millions of places at the same time. Jesus, bound by the flesh, could only be in one place at a time. His ability to be present everywhere at the same instant is part of what he "laid aside" when he came to live among us.

But his "body," the church, can be everywhere. We each serve Jesus as a part of his "body."

Ephesians 2:10

One final verse for today's conversation comes from the Apostle Paul. In Ephesians 2:8–9, Paul lays out how our salvation is something God created and delivers to us. Even the faith to believe in Jesus is given to us. Ephesians 2:1 begins by saying we were dead in our trespasses and sins. Dead people can't do much. But God (v. 4) made us alive (v. 5). It was not of our own doing but a gift from God (v.

8), not a result of works so that no one may boast (v. 9). Our salvation is God's work. Then he adds:

> For we are his workmanship, created in Christ
> Jesus for good works, which God prepared be-
> forehand, that we should walk in them.
> (Eph. 2:10)

God saves us and leaves us here to do good works so others will see Jesus.

Okay, you're a minister.
Now, get back to work!

Mike's Story Continued

Since I was already in the workplace when I started follow-ing Jesus, I thought I should ask God to put me into full-time ministry. Maybe you've tried to go into full-time ministry, too. I asked God repeatedly, and for a while, I didn't sense any answer. But after I learned these principles, the message I heard from the Holy Spirit changed. It was like he said, "Okay, you're a minister. Now, get back to work!"

Ministry in Today's Workplace

Because we're all called to be servants or ministers, regard-less of our job, I began to wonder what God wanted me to do today. What a "minister" did years ago isn't very rele-vant today. It seems today that people don't want their ideas confronted. If we suggest there's an absolute truth or that the Bible is without error, even our work friends may think we're crazy. Coworkers may be belligerently anti-Christian, and we've just never known. We don't know much about the faith of many we work with.

And growing numbers of Bible studies, books, podcasts, and sermons about "marketplace ministry" expose the complexity. It seems we have become more and more separated. Bridging the gap seems too complex. We get tempted to just keep our opinions to ourselves. How can we reach our coworkers, customers, vendors, and friends if they won't discuss spiritual topics with us?

Today, we must go to work. What can we do today? Should we just stay out of trouble until Sunday? Or do we need to be Bible scholars or accomplished professional debaters to share our faith with others?

At Follower of One, I discovered several ideas from scripture to enable workplace Christ-followers to minister every day. At Follower of One, an online community for marketplace Christ-followers, we've grouped the ideas into five daily activities. We believe any person can do these five activities as part of any job, in any workplace, at any time of day. And it doesn't matter if we live in a place where we're free to worship God or not.

1. Pray. Ask God for direction, ask him to bless others, and give him thanks.

2. Appreciate others. Show appreciation to others through what we think, say, and do.

3. Know what we believe. Think about and prepare to explain our faith reasonably.

4. Serve others. Do tangible things that cause others to wonder why we want to serve.

5. Speak for ourselves. When asked, explain our faith with gentleness and respect.

In the next five weeks, we will move through these activities, one idea per week. Discuss the weekly session with your group. Then, for the next five workdays, read and pray through the daily passage and act according to the day's action step. A space is provided to make notes after each day and at the end of each week.

Week One: Questions for Discussion

What do you do for a living?

Why do you think Jesus saved you?

Do you see church work, evangelism, and discipleship as higher callings than regular, everyday work like driving a truck, working in a call center, or selling a product? Why?

Why do you think Jesus left you here? Wouldn't heaven be a better place for you? What is it we can do here that we won't be able to do in heaven?

What "greater works" do you think Jesus was talking about in John 14:12? Did you notice any choice in John 14:12? Did Jesus say we might do the works? What does this have to do with "ministry" as you understand it?

What percentage of your time at work (or away from church activities) would you say is ministry? Do you hope to change that? What change would you like to see and why?

Is the answer above acceptable to you? If not, what would you like to do about it? What would your life look like if you were a full-time marketplace minister?

Action Steps for Week One

Week One, Day One

Passage:	Read Matthew 5:13–16 in more than one translation.
	"In the same way, let your light shine before others, so that they may see your good works and give glory to your Father who is in heaven." (Matt. 5:16)
Action:	Ask God to show you where you can be salt and light. What ideas come to mind? Share them with a friend and ask them what ideas they get. Then make notes. What can you change today to begin the process of living as a full-time minister? Take one of those actions this week.
Notes:	

Week One, Day Two

Passage:	Read Mark 10:35–45. "'What do you want me to do for you?' he asked." (Mark 10:36 NIV)
Action:	Ask God to show you how to serve others in your work context. Remember, this is a lowly job. What kinds of lowly jobs can you do to help others? What jobs never get done? Can you do one? Share your thoughts below.
Notes:	

Week One, Day Three

Passage:	Read John 13:1–16 and John 14:12. "Truly, truly, I say to you, whoever believes in me will also do the works that I do; and greater works than these will he do, because I am going to the Father." (John 14:12)
Action:	Washing feet was the lowest of the lowly jobs in that day. Has God given you any ideas as you have prayed over the last two days? Ask God to help you act on what he showed you yesterday and today. Act today. Make notes below about what you've done.
Notes:	

Week One, Day Four

Passage:	Read Ephesians 2:1–10. "For we are his workmanship, created in Christ Jesus for good works, which God prepared beforehand, that we should walk in them." (Eph. 2:10)
Action:	Ask God to show you the good works he has placed before you. Do you believe the Holy Spirit can give you five ideas? List them below. What good work comes to mind? Will you do it today?
Notes:	

Week One, Day Five

Passage:	Read Matthew 23:1–12. "Whoever exalts himself will be humbled, and whoever humbles himself will be exalted." (Matt. 23:12)
Action:	Ask Jesus to show you any areas where you aim for the chief seat or positions of authority. What deeds do you do to be noticed by men? Ask God to give you clear guidance on verse 11: "The greatest among you shall be your servant." Are you willing to climb God's corporate ladder? Who can you serve today? What does God have for you to do? And if you don't know, make it a point to listen to God and let him tell you.
Notes:	

Week One Additional Notes

Notes:	

Week Two

Pray

Leader's Notes

Begin the conversation this week, and future weeks, by reviewing how everyone did with the daily exercises. A key takeaway from this mission "trip" is to get in the habit of being "on-mission" while we're at work.

Make a big deal of the people who made notes each day. Talk a bit more about the challenges and encourage those who were unable to complete any of the daily assignments. Encourage and then encourage more.

Discuss ways to daily look at the verse and then make notes, maybe in the morning for the previous day or in the evening for the current day. This helps build the daily routine of praying for everyone we meet.

Finally, maybe you need to contact members of the group mid-week to ask how they're doing and to pray for the team. As the leader, your faithful prayer will make a difference!

Introduction

Why do we pray? Prayer is silly unless God is almighty (Luke 1:37), interested (Matthew 10:29–31), and active

(Matthew 6:25–30). But because God is almighty, interested, active, and more, praying makes great sense.

> Pray without ceasing. (1 Thess. 5:17)

> Do not be anxious about anything, but in everything by prayer and supplication with thanksgiving let your requests be made known to God. (Phil. 4:6)

Anxiety is experiencing failure in advance. But through prayer, we ask God to intervene. When we pray, we invite God into our situation.

Video

Begin by watching this video about the mission trip's first daily activity, prayer.

Three Types of Prayer

All prayer is beneficial. However, I've found three types of prayer to be particularly valuable as we interact with others as everyday workplace missionaries.

"Here I Am!"

The first prayer is, "Here I am!" Six people in the Bible responded this way to God. God called them, and they said, "Here I am," or "Here am I." Review the following verses and think about these stories and these people. They were:

1. Abraham (Genesis 22:1, 11)
2. Jacob (Genesis 31:11 and 46:2)
3. Moses (Exodus 3:4)
4. Samuel (1 Samuel 3:4–11)
5. Isaiah (Isaiah 6:8)
6. Ananias (Acts 9:10)

Many responded as if they said, "Here I am," but those words aren't recorded. These six are not exclusive, just special. In fact, in Revelation 3:20, Jesus extends the call to everyone. At the end of the letter to the church at Laodicea, Jesus says, "Behold, I stand at the door and knock."

When you say "Here I am!" in prayer each morning, you "punch in" and go to work with Jesus. He is active, working, and involved wherever you are today. He knocks on your door and the door of the people you will meet.

For Others

God has you in your workplace to serve others and treat them as more important than yourself. You show this by praying for them.

If you're like me, sometimes your prayers might be selfish. I have often prayed and asked Jesus to get me a new job or to make my present job better. I even prayed, "Get me out of here!" a few (several) times.

> ### But if God is almighty, we're not in our present job by accident. What's the best thing we can do in our current situation?

When you pray for others, you look for ways to join Jesus as he works in the lives of those around you. Even if you know very little about your coworker, you can ask God to bless them and use you to make a difference in their life.

> First of all, then, I urge that supplications, prayers, intercessions, and thanksgivings be made for all people, for kings and all who are in high positions, that we may lead a peaceful and quiet life, godly and dignified in every way. This is good, and it is pleasing in the sight of God our Savior, who desires all people to be saved and to come to the knowledge of the truth.
> (1 Tim. 2:1–4)

Jesus desires all people "to be saved and to come to the knowledge of the truth." So, pray for them. The best thing that could happen to any person you meet is that they would move a little closer to Jesus.

In fact, my working definition of the word "ministry" is just that: helping others move one notch closer to Jesus.

In the last lesson, we agreed that we're each called to serve. When we serve others so that they move closer to Jesus, that's Christian ministry.

Thanksgiving

Our third type of regular prayer in our workplaces is thanksgiving. One way we look different is when we give thanks to God for the not-so-good things that happen to us. If God is active, interested, and almighty, and something happens to us that we don't like, we have a choice. We can complain and express disappointment or anger, or we can thank God (1 Thess. 5:18). Since we know he is in charge, thanking him should be the logical response. But deep down inside, at least for me, I find it difficult to break the complaining habit. I still want to be my own god and pass judgment on my circumstances.

When I exercise thanksgiving to God for everything that happens, God becomes a bit more visible because my life is marked by a thankful, content heart.

The Consultant and the Bracelet

Scott was one of three consultants on a two-week consulting project. Being with a very large consulting firm, all three consultants were from different regions and wouldn't likely work together on a project again any time soon. He asked questions about both coworkers' faith, and the senior person seemed to be a Christ-follower, but the other person clearly stated they didn't believe in Christ. So he continued to pray for a way to discuss faith issues with the coworker. On the last night of the trip, he prayed with his wife on the phone, and they agreed that he would share his gospel bracelet, if possible, the next day. As they were entering the airport, he asked if the friend would like his bracelet, and the coworker said yes. As the coworker put the bracelet on, he asked about the colors, so Scott took the opportunity to share the gospel story using the bracelet. While the coworker received the presentation, Scott didn't know for sure if his coworker accepted Jesus or not. But Scott was encouraged and joyful because he trusted Jesus and acted on the leading he received.

Check out the Follower Of One Podcast at plnk.to/followerofone.

Week 2: Questions for Discussion

How often would you say you pray for people you see every day?

What would you pray for if you thought anything was possible?

Who comes to mind? Take a few minutes and let God give you ideas. Don't forget servers and service personnel.

How often would you say you pray for people while you're talking with them? What about before or after?

Think about how you pray for yourself. How can you make those same prayers for your coworkers, customers, or vendors?

List some ideas for how you can remember to pray for others. One idea is to set a daily reminder, maybe at 8:01 a.m., to remind you to pray for one another and your coworkers for the duration of this trip.

Pray

Action Steps for Week Two

Week Two, Day One

Passage:	Read Philippians 4:6-7, Revelation 3:20, and Isaiah 6:8.
	"I heard the voice of the Lord saying, 'Whom shall I send, and who will go for us?' Then I said, 'Here I am! Send me.'" (Isa. 6:8)
Action:	Ask God to show you how to do "everything by prayer" (Phil. 4:6). Thank him for knocking on your door (Rev. 3:20), and then tell him you're here to do his will (Isa. 6:8). Put yourself on the clock today. Now, what does he want you to do? Will you do what he says? Say it: "Here I am, Lord. Send me!"
Notes:	

Week Two, Day Two

Passage:	Read 1 Timothy 2:1–8. "First of all, then, I urge that requests, prayers, intercessions, and thanks be offered on behalf of all people." (1 Tim. 2:1 NET)
Action:	Today, pray for everyone you will interact with by name. Ask God to bless them. His blessing is powerful. And ask God to make you aware of ways you can cooperate with him as he blesses them. How does he want you to serve them? What can you do today? Do whatever comes to mind.
Notes:	

Week Two, Day Three

Passage:	Read Matthew 6:5–15. "Do not be like them, for your Father knows what you need before you ask him." (Matt. 6:8)
Action:	Pray again for the people on your calendar and near you at work. Ask God to guide you and change you as you pray. Other ideas may come to mind, but you don't have all the facts. What other information do you need to proceed? It could be that you need to know your coworkers or customers better. Make plans to spend extra time listening.
Notes:	

Week Two, Day Four

Passage:	Read Job 42:8 and 10.
	"The Lord also restored the fortunes of Job when he prayed for his friends, and the Lord increased double all that Job had." (Job 42:10 NASB)
Action:	The Lord instructed Job to pray for his friends, and when he did, God restored Job's fortune. Who have you forgotten to pray for? Ask God and pray for them, too. If anything comes to mind, write it down. And if not, keep praying until something comes to mind.
Notes:	

Week Two, Day Five

Passage:	Read Exodus 15:22–25. "And he cried to the LORD, and the LORD showed him a log, and he threw it into the water, and the water became sweet. There the LORD made for them a statute and a rule, and there he tested them." (Exod. 15:25)
Action:	Who does God bring to your mind when you pray? Is God asking you to pray for someone to make their situation better? Is He asking you to bless someone else? Ask God to make this obvious to you. What about your barista or mail carrier or the janitor at work? Who else can you pray for? If God puts something in your mind while you're praying, that may be an answer.
Notes:	

Week Two Additional Notes

Notes:	

Week Three

Appreciate Others

Leader's Notes

As you welcome everyone to the meeting, ask for a success story. This would be a story of something they experienced related to a recent prayer. Obedience and participation are success at this stage. The God of the universe is powerful, so when we join him, we experience his joy, and we make progress on the mission trip.

Even if we fail to see something miraculous, God is at work. Encourage others and help them discover their own ability to follow this plan of action. Make sure everyone feels welcome and willing to share. At the same time, ask God to encourage the mature believers to share their experiences and encourage others to stretch.

Then, before you start this lesson and watch the video, ask, "What types of activities or actions cause you to feel appreciated?"

Introduction

Do you see others as an obstacle, a distraction, or a necessary constraint to successfully advancing your career? Do you feel if you were left alone, you could do your work better? Or are you tempted, like me, to see people as resources? Are there some people you just fail to notice?

Video

Begin by watching the video "Appreciate Others."

Appreciation Equals Love

> *"Teacher, which is the great commandment in the Law?" And he said to him, "You shall love the Lord your God with all your heart and with all your soul and with all your mind. This is the great and first commandment. And a second is like it: You shall love your neighbor as yourself. On these two commandments depend all the Law and the Prophets."*
>
> —Matthew 22:36–40

Every person we meet is someone Jesus suffered and died to save. Jesus was asked by a Jewish religious leader what the greatest commandment was. And Jesus answered with two commands: love God and love others.

True love for another person is deliberately putting their needs ahead of our own. But since the word "love" is so broadly used, we can use appreciation as a code word. To appreciate others, we actively think about others and then act to make them successful.

Make Time

We have time to do things we consider important. If we knew Jesus would be feeding 5,000 people today or telling us to walk on water, we would make plans to be there. But Jesus seldom gives us his schedule in advance. So, if we want to see him work, we need to make time.

When we make time for others, we create room for appreciation. Most of us are too busy hurrying to get somewhere or do something.

Jennifer regularly makes new friends and finds opportunities to minister to others when she adds time into her schedule. One story involved a greeter at a retail store. Jennifer made time for the greeter and got to know them better. As a result, they ended up taking part in a regular Bible study and bringing others to the study too! God will fill the time you give him.

Also, our appreciation doesn't matter unless it's felt by someone else. When we make time for others, we demonstrate our appreciation because we treat others as more important than ourselves (Phil. 2:3).

At the same time, we must also guard and respect others' time. If we use their time without permission or try to appreciate them when they're busy with another matter, we create negative results.

For anyone, consider asking permission before taking their time. They may have an urgent issue and be unable to talk now. Ask them (and God) to find the best time and place to show appreciation.

And remember, if you have an employer, they have expectations of your time. Protect their investment. Come to work early or stay late so you can get ahead. This way, if a coworker needs something, you may be able to help because you're ahead of schedule.

Listen

Active listening is another way to show appreciation. Ask a question and then ask a follow-up question. Make it a point to look people in the eye and resist the temptation to look at people or things behind them. Trust Jesus enough to invest all your energy in the present conversation. And wait to think about what you're going to say next until they've stopped.

When we listen, we send the message we appreciate others.

This is difficult for me. I'm much more occupied with my own thoughts and ideas. Often, I begin searching my brain for responses before the other person completes their full idea or question. I may even interrupt or begin to respond to the wrong statement because I thought I knew what they were saying.

But you and I must remember that almost everyone has some history with our faith. Many people have been in conversations in which someone was determined to recite an entire gospel presentation to "help" them see the light. We've all been victims of someone who wants to say something no matter what.

But when we listen, we send the message we appreciate them. We don't bring an agenda other than to understand and serve the other person.

Remember What You Thought

Do you remember life before you trusted Jesus? Ephesians 2:1 says you were dead in your trespasses and sins. Do you remember what it was like to limit your approach to life to only the things you can see?

Consider Other's Beliefs

What might your coworkers believe? Do you have the courage to ask? Take a few minutes or even a lunch break with a coworker or friend and ask a few questions about their beliefs.

During the conversation, resist all temptations to argue or present your own ideas or offer your opinions. The point is to learn, not argue. Just listen and let God direct you on how you can appreciate your friend better because you learned more about their beliefs.

Speak

Another form of appreciation is to speak up. Sometimes we need to look someone in the eye and say, "Thank you!" Ask God to make you aware of how often you say "thank you" to others. Are you proud of the number? Try to increase the count. God will show you what others do for you. And when you respond, be specific. When you can be specific in your appreciation, others sense your genuine care. Think in advance for words and be as specific as possible.

Act

Your first daily activity from the last chapter was to pray for your friends. When you pray, you place your friends before God. Now, ask God to:

1. Give you genuine appreciation for them and specifics about what they do for you.

2. Show you how to make them feel appreciated.

God doesn't want any to live apart from him. He will give you a heart for others as you ask and act.

Write a thank-you note or give a gift card. Purchase a drink or a meal. Invite someone to lunch. Go out of your way to show others your appreciation.

Sometimes Jesus will give you an idea of how to appreciate others when or because you pray. Some ideas come with clear thoughts about how to proceed. Others start out feeling far-fetched.

In every case, do whatever Jesus tells you to do. Resist the temptation to rule an idea out or give up on it because you don't see a good way to achieve the goal. Ask Jesus to help you get the job done. We'll talk more about this in "Week Five: Serve Others."

Finally, in the book *The Five Languages of Appreciation in the Workplace*, authors Gary Smalley and Paul White detail five types, or languages, of appreciation. Four of those are most acceptable in the workplace: words of affirmation, quality time, acts of service, and tangible gifts. Ask God to show you ways to deliver these types of appreciation. *For further reading, check out the book mentioned above.*

The Dr. Pepper

Alex was leaving the office. Just before he left, he noticed the soft-drink vendor refilling the machine. One Dr. Pepper didn't fit in the machine, so the vendor left it out where anyone could grab it. Alex first thought, "Great! Now I can have my favorite soft drink for the ride home."

But because he was on the mission trip, it also occurred to him another coworker also loved Dr. Pepper. So, Alex left the drink on his coworker's desk and left for the day. The next day, another coworker who had seen the gesture asked Alex why he did that. Alex then had an opportunity to share how his faith and the mission trip motivated him to give the drink away rather than keep it for himself!

Week 3: Questions for Discussion

If your coworkers were going to thank you for something, would you appreciate spoken appreciation, acts of service, tangible gifts, like a lunch or an award, or quality time more?

Who do you need to thank?

What ideas about showing gratitude pop into your mind?

How else can you help others feel appreciated?

Do you notice that people prefer different appreciation languages? Your preferred method won't be the same as everyone else. Ask God who you need to thank. List them here.

For the next week, who will you thank and how? Write that below.

Then, share your goals with the others in your group and make sure to ask someone in the group to follow up with you.

Action Steps for Week Three

Week Three, Day One

Passage:	Read 1 Corinthians 13. "Love is patient and kind; love does not envy or boast; it is not arrogant…" (1 Cor. 13:4)
Action:	Ask God to show you where you excel and where you fall short in loving others. Could it be that you excel in patience, but you tend to be rude or selfish? Or maybe you have compassion but no patience. Ask God to show you what to work on, and then create one action item for today to respond to God's conviction.
Notes:	

Week Three, Day Two

Passage:	Read Mark 10:35–52. "They replied, 'Let one of us sit at your right and the other at your left in your glory.'" (Mark 10:37)
Action:	Notice the contrast between the questions James and John asked Jesus and the question Bartimaeus asked. What do you see? What kinds of questions do you ask others? What daily action will you take to ask one more question, like, "Would you tell me more?" or "What else?"
Notes:	

Week Three, Day Three

Passage:	Read Ephesians 2:1–4. "And you were dead in [your] trespasses and sins." (Eph. 2:1)
Action:	Do you remember being dead? (Eph. 2:1) What did you believe before you started following Jesus? Today, ask Jesus to direct you to someone and ask about their beliefs. Make notes below for your records so you can remember and pray for your friend.
Notes:	

Week Three, Day Four

Passage:	Read Proverbs 18:21. "Death and life are in the power of the tongue, and those who love it will eat its fruit."
Action:	Your words matter. When you recall details, you show people they're important. Ask God to give you a heart for everyone you meet. Ask for ideas to help you remember names and details. These people are your ministry. What ideas and what people did you practice listening to today?
Notes:	

Week Three, Day Five

Passage:	Read Luke 9:12–17, especially verse 13. "You give them something to eat." (Luke 9:13)
Action:	Jesus asks the disciples to feed 5,000 people, but the disciples have no food. What do you have that you can give? Give something away. Pay for a meal of someone behind you in the drive-through. Or give a big tip. Get the name of a server and tell them what their service meant to you. Take time to notice others and help them. Then, note below what happened, what you thought, and how God directed you.
Notes:	

Week Three Additional Notes

Notes:	

Week Four

Know What You Believe

Leader's Notes

Welcome everyone to the meeting today and ask how their appreciation went last week. Again, check and ask if someone has a story to share related to anything about the mission trip so far.

Encourage others again this week, too. You will help them discover their own ability to follow this plan of action. Even if they missed all five days, get them to commit to doing the exercise tomorrow. Our willingness to pursue God and keep on asking, seeking, and knocking is the single factor in the formula for success.

Then, after an initial warm-up, ask participants to explain in one or two sentences, "Why do you follow Jesus?" Give time to share their answers. Next, we'll be working together to develop and share our answers to that key question.

Introduction: Why Do You Follow Jesus?

Most people work hard to get ahead in their careers. Everyone in the typical workplace understands the personal motivation to get ahead. But when someone works hard so they can help and serve others, our coworkers don't understand that motive nearly as well. It just doesn't add up.

Each time you go beyond what is expected, simply because you follow Jesus and want to serve others, some of the people around you may get curious. Eventually, you may be asked, "Why are you doing this?"

Video

Check out this video about the importance of being able to explain why we follow Jesus.

First Marketplace Minister

Jesus commissioned a (possibly the first) marketplace minister in Mark 5:1–20. First, he healed the man of demon possession. But because of the spectacle this caused, the local people asked Jesus to leave the area. As Jesus was leaving, the healed man asked if he could go with Jesus, but Jesus told him no. "Go home to your people and report to them what great things the Lord has done for you, and how He had mercy on you" (Mark 5:19 NASB). With nothing more than a one-sentence training session, Jesus sends him alone into a land where no one else knows or follows Jesus.

What Has Jesus Done for You?

Can you "report to them what great things the Lord has done for you and how He had mercy on you?" Your first question may come in another form. "Don't you have something better to do?" "Why would you stay late and help me?" "Why did you buy treats?" "Why are you asking me to forgive you for gossiping?"

The Natural Response

The natural response isn't to present the Gospel or invite someone to church. A natural response would be to answer for yourself. Why *are* you doing this?

When you answer that question, would someone else understand your reasoning? Or would they need to be a Christ-follower with a similar background and experience?

Often, people answer that question with a statement like, "Because Jesus loves me." I've heard others say they follow Jesus "because he died on the cross for my sins."

For those who don't follow Jesus, an explanation like those above seems strange. They're not likely to change their opinion about Jesus based on those explanations. They don't understand.

I chose to follow Jesus when I was 30 years old. I remember what I thought before I followed him. And I would have mentally discounted and discarded those "churchy" explanations from even my best friends.

Other Forms of the Question

Another question we hear is "Why are you doing this?" When you stay late to help a coworker with no reward or when you go out of your way to serve others, they won't understand your motives. For some, you will get an opportunity to explain your faith, but like first impressions, first explanations matter.

Therefore, we suggest participants practice answering these two questions: "Why are you doing this?" and "Why do you follow Jesus?" And we recommend four key principles for your response.

Four Keys

1. First, the answer needs to be genuine. Begin by writing out your answer to each question like you're answering someone who doesn't know who Jesus is or what he has done.

2. Use "I" and "me" statements. Try to answer the question you're asked. Most people won't ask you for a gospel presentation or how to get to heaven. They'll ask why you're doing this act of service. So, make sure your answers use "I" and "me" statements.

3. Include Jesus. Hopefully, your action was initiated because you follow Jesus. Then make sure to give him the credit. You're not doing

this because you're a good person. You're doing this because Jesus transformed you and gave you the job of helping others to know and follow him. So, make sure the person who asks you knows that Jesus was involved.

4. Make your answer somewhat brief. Try to keep it to a couple of sentences. Your answer will give them the first seed. God will direct you in your answer, and he will also prompt them to ask you more.

I generally say, "I'm doing this because my life changed when I began following Jesus. He went way out of his way for me, and so I try to go out of my way to help others."

Practice Makes Perfect

Then, practice. That's right. Get with another believer, maybe someone else at your workplace, and take turns asking and answering the question. Ask for their perspective on your answer and give them your thoughts on their answer. The more you practice, the more comfortable and natural you will be when you're asked.

Five Whys

Finally, when your partner gives you the answer, then follow with "But why?" Can they answer you intelligently if you ask, "Why?" five times? Those who will ask will genuinely want to know. Think about your answer in advance to show them respect. Make sure your answer is sincere, clear, reasonable, well thought out, and brief. They can choose to ask for more details if they have additional questions. And the Holy Spirit will work in their mind when your answers are clear.

Week Four: Exercises for Discussion

Instead of simple discussion questions, this week requires a bit of an exercise. If your group is more than four, break into sub-groups of no more than three people each. Take turns following these steps:

Step 1: Imagine you just bought someone's lunch or went out of your way to help a coworker. They ask, "Why are you doing this?" Share your answer here or with your group.

Step 2: Now, improve it. Someone in the group should ask, "But why?" Now what do you say? State your answer more clearly.

Step 3: But why? Go ahead, write out the next answer.

Step 4: But why? Again, write or share your answer.

Step 5: But why?

Did you get clearer as you went? Do you have a good feel for how to answer this question so that Jesus is part of the answer?

If you took the exercise above by yourself, share it with your friends when you meet. Or if you were in a breakout session, get back together and compare notes. What did you learn? Did you get any ideas? Take a few minutes to share what you learned and pray for one another. This is where your relationship with Jesus shows up in the world.

Step 6: Write a brief prayer to God asking for clarity. Thank him for making himself known to you, too.

Action Steps for Week Four

Week Four, Day One

Passage:	Read 1 Thessalonians 5:16–18.
	"Rejoice always, pray without ceasing, in everything give thanks; for this is the will of God for you in Christ Jesus." (NASB)
Action:	Today, practice rejoicing about everything that happens at work, both good and bad. And pray for your coworkers, customers, and vendors. Ask God to show you who you're forgetting or overlooking. Who else can you pray for? Write any ideas you get while you pray, and consider those as action items!
Notes:	

Week Four, Day Two

Passage:	Read Mark 5:1–20. Focus on verses 19–20. "And he did not permit him but said to him, 'Go home to your friends and tell them how much the Lord has done for you, and how he has had mercy on you.' And he went away and began to proclaim in the Decapolis how much Jesus had done for him, and everyone marveled." (Mark 5:19-20)
Action:	Write out your answer to why you follow Jesus. Think about and begin listing the "great things" God has done for you. Lookup a definition for the word "mercy." How has God had mercy on you? Then, pray for your coworkers today on the way to work. Ask God to show you who you need to get to know better.
Notes:	

Week Four, Day Three

Passage:	Read Colossians 4:5–6. "Conduct yourself with wisdom toward outsiders, making the most of the opportunity." (Col. 4:5 NASB)
Action:	Get treats for the office or invite someone to lunch, your treat. Do anything over and above the call of your job. And practice answering the question, "Why do you follow Jesus?" Think about your answer and help a friend with theirs.
Notes:	

Week Four, Day Four

Passage:	Read Colossians 3:1–11. "Set your mind on the things that are above, not on the things that are on earth. For you have died, and your life is hidden with Christ in God." (Col. 3:2–3 NASB)
Action:	Continue praying for others and practice your answers again. Consider asking someone else if they ever think about spiritual things. Ask for their opinion without offering your own. Ask to learn. And write a thank you note or give someone a special "thank you" gift. Try to extend your regular practice further as you set your mind on things above.
Notes:	

Week Four, Day Five

Passage:	Read Colossians 3:12–17.
	"Whatever you do in word or deed, do everything in the name of the Lord Jesus, giving thanks through Him to God the Father." (Col. 3:17 NASB)
Action:	As you pray for your coworkers today, ask God to bring someone to you who asks about the hope they see in you. And if he gives you an idea during or after your prayer time, figure out a way to do it. Stay late and help someone in their job or come in early to help out. When God gives you an idea, act.
Notes:	

Week Four Additional Notes

Notes:	

Week Five

Serve Others

Leader's Notes

After your initial welcome, again, ask how the last week went. Did your companions get a chance to work on their one- or two-sentence explanation? Ask them to share it with the group.

Does anyone have a story to share related to anything about the mission trip so far? Are there any updates on prayer requests or health issues? Make sure to stay connected personally. Don't just focus on this lesson. Always make time for encouragement and prayer for one another. Then review individual involvement. Are members practicing the daily activities with more frequency?

Before you move into the next section, ask people, "What do you do on a regular basis that you wish you could hire someone else to do?" What kinds of answers do you get? Talk for a minute about their most disliked activities each week. Then they'll be ready to talk about serving others.

Introduction

God uses us to serve others. Jesus came to seek and to save the lost (Luke 19:10). He announced the kingdom of heaven is at hand (Matt. 4:17, Mark 1:15). He taught us to ask for God's kingdom. But his method was service.

> For even the Son of Man did not come to be served, but to serve, and to give his life a ransom for many. (Mark 10:45 NASB)

In this passage, Jesus is responding at the end of a discussion that took place a few verses earlier. The disciples were arguing (again) about who would be greatest in Jesus's kingdom. But Jesus stated that we must enter the kingdom like a child and that the top position in the kingdom of God was the position of a servant.

Video

Take a few minutes and watch this video in which Mike talks about our calling to serve others.

Servant Versus King

Jesus prepares a place for us (John 14:2–3), but it won't be our kingdom. When we follow Jesus, he asks us to give up our right to ourselves, which is difficult. We want to keep some of our own kingdom for ourselves. We want to choose what we think, eat, or watch. But God's kingdom doesn't include our kingdom. Jesus laid down his life.

> And he said to all, "If anyone would come after me, let him deny himself and take up his cross daily and follow me. For whoever would save his life will lose it, but whoever loses his life for my sake will save it." (Luke 9:23–24)

Jesus came to serve, and he calls us to serve. When we serve, we make him visible. The original temptation to Adam and Eve in Genesis 3:5 was to have our eyes opened and be like God, knowing good and evil. We wanted our own kingdom. We didn't want to be in God's kingdom. And every one of us has made the same choice (Rom. 3:23).

Get Outside Your Job Description

Before we follow Jesus, we work for our own kingdom, and we think everyone else does, too. On the surface, our life doesn't look different from others. But, when we serve others without building a kingdom of our own, our lives uncover a different reality. Jesus becomes visible.

Our service to others won't be noticeable until it is outside of our job description. That doesn't mean we try and do our boss's job or someone else's job. And it doesn't mean we mind other's business or try to tell them how to do their job.

Four Facets of Activity Outside Our Job Description

When we "get outside of our job description," we mean:

1. Do your job very well—so well that those who depend on you are blown away.

2. Do your excellent work early. Work done in advance will matter when someone else needs help. You won't have to tell them you're too busy to help. Go above the normal call of duty early so you can be interrupted and have the time and ability to help.

3. Serve others outside of a work context. Once I had to take a coworker's wife home from a hospital stay. Ask God to show you and listen to find needs and then offer humbly to help where possible.

4. Stay humble. Your service is for Christ. We give away our rights for his reasons because of what he did for us. Avoid doing anything to be noticed. Serve others because Jesus will know. What we do in secret will be rewarded (Matt. 6:1).

Others have little desire to learn about our faith because they don't see the generosity, grace, peace, life, and joy in our lives. We look like many other people who don't follow Jesus. But, when we bring humble generosity beyond the normal, the Holy Spirit will use our service and cause others to see (glorify) God (Matt. 5:16). When we live in God's holy joy from being obedient and generous, that's cheerful giving (2 Cor. 9:7).

The Video Game

Jennifer and Kevin wanted to give a friend a gift, and they decided to purchase a copy of a video game they knew their friend wanted. But the game was out of production, and they were having trouble finding one. A nearby game store website showed having the game in stock, but they couldn't make the purchase, and the reason was unclear.

As they continued to pray about this effort, they decided to go to the store. After some time, the store employee found the game. It had been reserved *two years earlier* by someone who never picked it up! So, the store sold the game to Jennifer and Kevin, who were overjoyed at how God had reserved this game for their friend for two years. Additionally, they told the whole story to the store employees during the encounter, too!

Let God Lead

Don't give under compulsion but ask God to show you how and when to serve others. Be willing to give, not just generously but dangerously, like the widow in Mark 12:42–44. Give beyond what you're able to give. Then, trust him for the joy you will receive when you give dangerously. Time and energy for many are in shorter supply than money. So,

ask God what you can give and then move when he gives
you an idea.

Week Five: Questions for Discussion

Most people will accept help when they're certain you have no ulterior motive. What ideas come to mind when you think about ways to serve others?

Ask God to give you three more ideas and write those here.

Make a commitment. What action will you take by when?

Will you make room in your monthly budget and schedule to buy lunch or coffee for a coworker?

What things can you do to improve your job performance?

Action Steps for Week Five

Week Five, Day One

Passage:	Read Mark 2:1–13. Think about how the friends of the paralyzed man acted. Are you ready to climb up on the roof to lower your friend in front of Jesus?
Action:	Begin this week praying for others again. How can you serve them? Let God guide you with ideas for how to serve others. Take note of any ideas. Which ones do you commit to completing this week?
Notes:	

Week Five, Day Two

Passage:	Read 2 Corinthians 9:6. "Now I say this: the one who sows sparingly will also reap sparingly, and he who sows generously will also reap generously." (NASB)
Action:	Today, as you pray around your workplace or for the people on your calendar, ask God to show you who to serve. Everything you give matters. Get a gift card for a coworker. Or give a $50 tip for your morning coffee. Do something extreme, trusting God to use it. Make notes below about your action.
Notes:	

Week Five, Day Three

Passage:	Read 2 Corinthians 9:7.
	"Each one must do just as he has decided in his heart, not reluctantly or under compulsion, for God loves a cheerful giver." (NASB)
Action:	This is your service week. Who else can you serve? Who did you think of today that you hadn't thought of yet? What else can you do? Record your notes from today's activity.
Notes:	

Week Five, Day Four

Passage:	Read 2 Corinthians 9:8. "And God is able to make all grace overflow to you, so that, always having all sufficiency in everything, you may have an abundance for every good deed." (NASB)
Action:	Remember again to pray for everyone you will meet. Then, take some action. Have you purchased treats for the break room this week? If you're running low on ideas, commit to spending ten extra minutes today listening with the Holy Spirit to the people you interact with. What other ideas do they give you? What other needs do you hear about? Make notes and take action.
Notes:	

Week Five, Day Five

Passage:	Read John 15:1–17. "I am the vine, you are the branches; the one who remains in Me, and I in him bears much fruit, for apart from Me you can do nothing." (John 15:5 NASB)
Action:	Abide means to live with. Live with Jesus today and let him direct you. Focus on why you follow Jesus. Ask him to show you how to demonstrate his peace in your circumstances. Look around. Pray for people. Note below who you served and how. What can you do next week, too?
Notes:	

Week Five Additional Notes

Notes:	

Week Six

Speak for Yourself

Leader's Notes

After your initial welcome, again, ask how the last week went. Did they serve others, and how was the service received? Does anyone have a story to share related to anything about the mission trip so far? Are there any updates on prayer requests or health issues? Remember to make time for encouragement and prayer and review individual involvement. Are members practicing the daily activities with more frequency?

Then, before you move into the next section, ask people, "Have you ever been in a situation where someone else drove the conversation and wouldn't shut up?" Spend a few moments feeling the frustration of that type of experience. You might even pray for those people who just won't stop talking. After thinking about this type of unpleasant situation, hopefully, everyone will be ready to talk about speaking for themselves.

Concern About Speaking Up

Many Christians express concern when it comes to conversations with others about Jesus. It is rude to inject religion or politics into conversations. Often, people believe religion and politics are both based on opinions. Our coworkers and friends chose to come to work today to make a living, not have a religious discussion. When we're at work, we should focus on work, not on faith.

Video

Take a minute and watch this video about how we speak with others about our faith. Remember, because we're in a short-term mission trip context, this isn't designed to be fully comprehensive. Rather this approach is designed to maintain relationships and cause others to think about their own faith.

Unequipped

You may believe you're not equipped or allowed to talk about faith at work. Many of us have heard about training to "present the gospel." Maybe you've even taken such training. If you haven't taken the training, you may feel un-qualified.

Manipulation

And even if you have taken the training, you know it is rude to try and engineer a conversation so you can "share the gospel." I know when someone is steering a conversation, and I don't like the idea that I must steer the conversation either.

> *None of us is perfect, so some degree of error must be acceptable.*

Conversations with Other Christians

Many of us won't even talk about our faith with others who follow Jesus. We don't want to risk starting a discussion about non-core issues like speaking in tongues or once-saved-always-saved. I say "non-core" because the core issue is whether we try to follow Jesus. None of us is perfect, so some degree of error must be acceptable. If we follow Jesus, let's do everything we can to live at peace with all men (Romans 12:16–18).

People Will Ask

We don't need to manipulate conversations. Peter tells us people will ask:

> But in your hearts revere Christ as Lord. Always be prepared to give an answer to everyone who asks you to give the reason for the hope that you have. But do this with gentleness and respect… (1 Pet. 3:15 NIV)

Peter says we should prepare to give an answer to everyone who asks. When we serve others outside of our job description, people will be confused. Some will ask. We might be tempted to give them the answer before they ask the question. But God is already calling them to a relationship. He is busy using everything in their lives to draw them to himself. Your service is one of those things God uses.

Our Hope

In God's timing, especially if we follow the first four daily activities, others will ask us about our motives. We should be prepared to answer. We began working on our answer in week four. Our answer is "the reason for the hope that [we] have."

What hope? The hope that we received when we began to follow Jesus (Rom. 5:1–5). We follow him because we experience that hope now when the Holy Spirit uses us to make Jesus visible. This is the hope that causes us to do this study or to take part in the daily activities (pray, appreciate others, know what we believe, serve others, and speak for ourselves). Others see the difference in our lives as a glimpse of that hope.

Joy

When we trust God and follow him, we practice these first four activities. We pray for others and appreciate them. We think about what we believe, so we're prepared to give an answer, and then we actively serve others with joy.

Joy is what God gives us when we obey him. Even a painful job for ungrateful people can be a source of joy when we do it for God. Our joy becomes noticeable, and joy is contagious.

People like to be around joyful people. They "enjoy" people of joy. Our joy comes from God when we obey him. That's how Paul can command us to "rejoice in the Lord always; again I will say, rejoice" (Phil. 4:4).

Done for You

In lesson four, we discussed the first marketplace missionary. Jesus cast an army of demons out of him. When Jesus was leaving the region, the man asked if he could come with Jesus.

> But Jesus did not permit him to do so. Instead, he said to him, "Go to your home and to your people and tell them what the Lord has done for you, that he had mercy on you." (Mark 5:19 NET)

Jesus tells the man to stay with his people, his family, and friends and tell them "what the Lord has done for you, that he had mercy on you." This one personal command is all we have recorded of the instruction Jesus gave the man.

With this one sentence of training, Jesus left this man in a community that ignored God. He had no support network that we're aware of, but he did have a story of what Jesus did for him.

Your Story

You have a story too. What has Jesus done for you? We practiced this back in chapter four, but more practice will help. Peter tells us to "always be prepared to give an answer" (1 Pet. 3:15 NIV).

People will ask why you're different. When they ask, give them your story. Speak for yourself. Let them process your answer and compare it to their life and their experience in their own time. Let the Holy Spirit do his work. Your answer is the seed. Every seed takes time before it grows.

If your story doesn't use "I" and "me" statements, then it may be a lecture. Speak for yourself by using "I" and "me" statements. Remember to report what the Lord has done for you and how he had mercy on you.

Week Six: Questions for Discussion

What has the Lord done for you?

Do you naturally answer that question using "I" and "me" statements?

Write your answers to "Why are you doing this?" and "Why do you follow Jesus?" below.

What can you do to make those answers more conversational?

Take turns discussing these answers among your small group. Write anything that comes to mind.

Ask God to bless others and prompt them to ask. Ask him to give you ideas for how you can serve them better. And then wait. This will take time. Continue to serve others and pray for them so they will ask.

Action Steps for Week Six

Week Six, Day One

Passage:	Read Luke 8:26–39. "'Return to your home, and declare how much God has done for you.' And he went away, proclaiming throughout the whole city how much Jesus had done for him." (Luke 8:39)
Action:	This is another version of the story of the man who wanted to go with Jesus. Jesus told him to stay. What do you notice that's different? The command is slightly different. Today, practice your answer to this question. Has anyone asked yet? Don't give up. Keep praying, doing what God tells you to do, and be ready to answer in the first person.
Notes:	

Week Six, Day Two

Passage:	Read 1 Corinthians 9:24–27. "But I strictly discipline my body and make it my slave, so that, after I have preached to others, I myself will not be disqualified." (1 Cor. 9:27 NASB)
Action:	Today, as you pray, ask God to show you where you need discipline. Then do what he says. Can you improve the quality of your work or refrain from gossip? Do you need to pray for people you don't particularly like? Ask God to show you. And make sure you follow through praying for others and doing things for them, too.
Notes:	

Week Six, Day Three

Passage:	Read Genesis 32:27–30 and Philippians 2:9–11. "Therefore God exalted him to the highest place and gave him the name that is above every name." (Phil. 2:9 NIV)
Action:	Do you remember names? Names are important to God and to us. You like to hear your name. Today, practice saying names more. If you need help remembering names, use them more, and you'll remember them better. Ask someone to tell you about their spouse or kids. Make notes, too. Plan to ask about that person by name again tomorrow.
Notes:	

Week Six, Day Four

Passage:	Read Philippians 3:7–16. "But whatever gain I had, I counted as loss for the sake of Christ." (Phil. 3:7)
Action:	Give a gift or purchase snacks for the office again. In addition to praying for the people you will see, do something out of the ordinary for someone. Did you learn a new name or two yesterday? Make a point of saying their name in conversation. "Hey, Mike! How are you doing?" Then also mention the family member from yesterday. And if you've forgotten their name, admit it and ask them to help you remember. Make plans to use names. The more intentional you are about remembering names, the easier it will get.
Notes:	

Week Six, Day Five

Passage:	Read Ephesians 3:14–21, especially verse 20.
	"Now to Him who is able to do far more abundantly beyond all that we ask or think, according to the power that works within us…" (Eph. 3:20 NASB)
Action:	This passage sums up the mission trip. According to God's riches, we are strengthened with his power through his Spirit (v. 16). This is so Jesus would be present, or dwell, with us in our hearts through faith. Our foundation is love—his love for us and our love for the brothers. Because of his love (v. 17) received by us and shown by us, we can understand our position (v. 18), know his love, and be filled. Our fullness in Christ is what others notice. That's our joy. When they see it, they will ask. Everyone wants that fullness that only Jesus offers. Meditate on this today as you pray for your friends and coworkers.
Notes:	

Week Six Additional Notes

Notes:	

Next Steps

Congratulations!

Did you experience God's joy as you obeyed him during this "trip?" Most who complete the trip say they want to keep it going. Do you?

Whether you want to keep it going or not, would you please give us your feedback? Scan the QR code to check out our resources page and complete the feedback form. There's also a video to help you choose your next steps.

Not What You Thought?

Did the trip meet your expectations? If not, why not? Many people experience a sense of let-down. They didn't see God much. They expected more. Many experience serious spiritual warfare during this event. Did you think, "This isn't making any difference; why am I trying this?"

Ask God for direction. If you think this trip can be improved, please let us know by sending a note to our feedback mailbox: feedback@followerofone.org. You may also want to take the trip again. God always works to help us grow our faith and trust. He will use your discomfort to help you grow your reliance on him if you cooperate. He always works for our best.

Enjoyable Experience?

If the trip met or exceeded your expectations, keep it going. This doesn't have to be a one-time experience. The changes you made during this "trip" won't become permanent in your life unless you put down a landmark. Like Joshua who set up 12 stones in the Jordan to mark the place where the Israelites crossed the Jordan on dry ground (Joshua 4:8), you need to mark this change in your life and environment.

Recommended Action Steps: Find Out More on Our Resources Page

1. Commit. Tell God your thoughts. Ask him to make clear what you should do next. Do whatever he says.

2. Give us your feedback.

3. Join our online community to keep your trip going.

4. Pay it forward. A contribution in any amount will be a blessing to our ministry. An ongoing contribution of as little as $10 a month will cement marketplace ministry in your life and pay for others to experience it too.

5. Take the mission trip again. You can take the two-week version of this trip in our online community. After you log in to the community, go to our courses and request access for the next marketplace mission trip.

6. Or get more copies of this book for some other friends and lead them through the trip.

Questions for Reflection

What moments would I like to remember about this mission trip?

How has this experience changed me? What did I learn?

What ideas did God give me that need to become part of my regular work week?

What things would I do differently? Can I put any of those ideas into action today?

Do I honestly want Jesus to guide me during my workday?

What will I do to keep this mission trip going? Will I put a note on my calendar for a few weeks from today to reflect on this exercise more?

Final Thoughts

Every day, wherever you go, Jesus is present. We train our minds and our bodies to intentionally be aware of his presence, his power, and his love for us. Your mission is wherever you are. Take part in your mission and experience the joy of working with Jesus for the rest of your life.

> *"Behold, I stand at the door and knock; if anyone hears My voice and opens the door, I will come in to him and will dine with him, and he with Me."*
>
> —Jesus, Revelation 3:20 NASB

Thank you for the difference you've made.

Mike.- -

Follower Of One, Inc. is an Oklahoma corporation approved as a non-profit organization under section 501(c)(3) of the Internal Revenue Code.

Follower Of One, Inc.
mike@followerofone.org
followerofone.org
PO Box 101, Owasso, OK 74055
(918) 401-0011

Links: Follower of One

Learn more about Follower of One and our resources
using any of these links below:

1. Online Community:
   community.followerofone.org

2. Resources Page:

   followerofone.org/wbresources

3. Public Website: followerofone.org

4. YouTube Channel:
   www.youtube.com/c/FollowerofOne

5. Subscribe to Our Podcast:
   plnk.to/followerofone

6. LinkedIn Page: www.linkedin.com/com-
   pany/Follower-of-one

7. Facebook Page: facebook.com/followerofone

Links: Mike Henry Sr.

Here are a few ways you can connect with Mike Henry Sr., too!

1. Website: mikehenrysr.com

2. LinkedIn: www.linkedin.com/in/mikehenrysr

3. Facebook: facebook.com/mikehenrysr

4. Twitter: twitter.com/mikehenrysr

Join our Online Community

Follower of One is a community of leaders who follow Jesus. We want to live genuine lives of authentic influence as leaders who follow Jesus full-time.

1.

No Cost to join. Members donate to "Pay it forward".

2.

Take a 2-week daily version of the Mission Trip with people from all over the world.

3.

Get around others who want their faith to matter every day.

4.

Meet others with similar occupations or interests

5.

Connect with people from all over the globe.

6.

Join prayer calls and community calls

7.

Find out about local meetings and other events as they happen.

8.

Subscribe to our YouTube channel.

www.followerofone.org

@followerofone

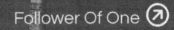

Invest in Follower Of One

Help build a community of Christ-followers who live genuine lives of authentic influence wherever they are

Exploration is a big part of what we do. Each person must figure out how they live their faith in their situation. There is no one size-fits-all solution!

As individuals and groups take part in the community, donations pay it forward so others can join, and explore, too!

Partners invest over and above individual and group giving to enable us to grow this unique ministry.

Individuals, groups and partners are needed to grow this community and mobilize the body of Christ.

Take part in building something new! Contact us to learn more.

www.followerofone.org

@followerofone